I BELIEVE
IN THE
BIBLE

I BELIEVE
IN THE BIBLE

Joseph R. Sizoo

ABINGDON PRESS
New York • *Nashville*

I BELIEVE IN THE BIBLE

Copyright © MCMLVIII by Abingdon Press

Library of Congress Catalog Card Number: 58-9525

SET UP, PRINTED, AND BOUND BY THE
PARTHENON PRESS, AT NASHVILLE,
TENNESSEE, UNITED STATES OF AMERICA

CONTENTS

CHAPTER ONE

A CONFESSION OF FAITH

I BELONG TO THOSE FORTUNATE GROUPS OF PEOPLE WHO were brought up on the Bible. In the formative years of my life I never lived beyond the sight and sound of that Book. In my boyhood home after each meal some sentences were read out of it. On Sunday evenings at twilight time, as the shadows lengthened, my father would gather us together and we would sing the hymns of our faith, after which my father would read to us out of the Book and expound it. The Psalmody of David, the matchless fifty-fifth chapter of Isaiah, the incomparable parables of Jesus, the unforgettable stories of providence, the love story of Ruth, the visions of the prophets, and the Apocalypse of John were part of my day-by-day life. "Come unto me, all ye that labour"; "God so loved the world, that he gave his only begotten Son"; "The Lord is my Shepherd; I shall not want"; "By grace are ye saved through faith"; "If with all your hearts ye truly seek me"—these were household sentences in the home of my childhood.

I do not recall all that as a depressing experience. I felt no sense of hardship or severity or resentment toward it. Indeed, I thought myself a fortunate boy growing up in that kind of home, and I look back upon it now as a blessed heritage. I would rather have the memory of those ex-

7

periences than all the bags of gold you can drag through Wall Street.

The Bible is the source book of culture

Then, too, I was brought up to believe that the Bible is the source book of all that is best in culture, philosophy, and wisdom. Bach and Beethoven, Haydn and Handel, were steeped in its truth. Rubens and Raphael, Titian and Tintoretto, Watts and Hoffman, turned to it for their themes. Milton, Dante, Tennyson, Browning, and Bunyan found in it their inspiration. Webster, Pitt, and Burke gained persuasive powers and oratorical abilities because of their familiarity with the laws of Moses and the prophet Isaiah. All the great of earth from Paul to Lincoln have gone forth as knights-errant upon their crusades of righteousness and compassion with their "feet shod with the preparation of the gospel." Countries where democracy has made its greatest impact have always had the open Book, known and read by all people.

There is nothing quite so significant as the growth of the Bible in the affection of the people of the earth. A little more than four hundred years ago William Tyndale translated the entire New Testament into the language of the plowman and later added portions of the Old Testament to the monumental enterprise. His generation rewarded him for this selfless act by strangling him to death, seizing the three-hundred-odd copies, burning them in public, leaving only one charred fragment to posterity. Today that Book is translated into more than eleven hundred languages or dialects of the modern world. The first public school was founded by the colonists in Massachusetts that the Bible might be taught the children, for, they said, "What avails freedom of religion if our children are ignorant of the Bible?" The first college was founded on our shores that young men might be trained to spread the story of that Book to the native people of the land. The Bible has fulfilled its prophecy: Its "line is gone out through all the earth," and its "words to the end of the world."

It would be difficult to measure the contribution that the Bible has made to the culture of the world. There is no finer poetry, no richer drama, no lovelier romance, no more intriguing biography anywhere in literature than that of the Bible. If you should take out of the culture of today all that the Bible has contributed, it would be like walking through a wheat field after a cyclone had swept over it and hailstones had beaten down the grain.

No literature will ever excel the haunting loveliness of the twenty-third psalm, the simple grandeur of the Sermon on the Mount, the appealing humanity of Luke's Gospel, the resonant eloquence of Isaiah, the matchless love story of Ruth, the superb visions of Revelation, the heroic tale of Esther, the incomparable beauty of the parables, and the lyric poetry of the Nunc Dimittis. John Winthrop wrote, "Diffuse the Bible and all else will follow"; while Immanuel Kant added, "It is the greatest benefaction which has ever come to human experience." Mohammed wrote one day in scorn that "Christians are people of the Book." That was an unwitting and glorious tribute to the Christian fellowship.

Its words are part of our life

I was also brought up to believe that the language of the Bible had entered into our day-by-day life. A knowledge of the Bible would enlarge and enrich my vocabulary. There are certain phrases and sentences current in our daily speech which have no meaning apart from that Book. We speak of the salt of the earth, a mess of pottage, a labor of love, the valley of decision, a drop in the bucket, the apple of the eye, a wolf in sheep's clothing, a house divided against itself, sweeter than honey, clear as crystal, wise as serpents. What are these but tiny phrases out of the Book? You see, I was brought up to know and revere the Book.

Through the long years of my life this Book has been, indeed, a "lamp unto my feet, and a light unto my path." I have tried to saturate my language with its vocabulary, my mind with its truth, my heart with its love, my conscience with its laws, and my life with its spirit. What it did for me, it will do for all: lift horizons, push back foothills, and give courage to live unashamed and unafraid.

CHAPTER **TWO**

THE WITNESS OF THE AGES

WHAT IS THIS BOOK WHICH HAS HAD SUCH A PROFOUND influence upon my life and on the lives of countless men and women everywhere? The word "Bible" is not itself a biblical word. It comes from the Greek by way of the Latin and means "little books." The name is derived from the Phoenician city Byblos, from which papyrus, the inner bark of the papyrus reed used for writing purposes, was exported. The word "Bible" was not applied to the sacred books until at least A.D. 400. Sometime in the thirteenth century the simple name "The Book" came into use. The use of the singular instead of the plural is important. It points to the fact that amid the diversity of authorship there is a basic unity. It clearly indicates that all wrote under the guidance of one great Spirit.

How are the books put together?

The books are not arranged in the order in which they were written. It is generally agreed by scholars that the earliest piece of prose writing in the Old Testament was the story of the founding of the Kingdom which is contained in the books of Samuel. In all probability the first book of the Old Testament to be accepted as sacred literature was the book of Deuteronomy, which actually stands fifth. So also, the first letter to the Thessalonians was the first book of the New Testament to be written, but it stands thirteenth. The Gospel of John, which stands fourth, was among the last to be written.

How did we get our Bible?

How did we get our Bible? The answer to this question forms an entrancing story. As we have seen, the Bible was a product of the centuries. It is the witness of the ages manifested in and through history. Perhaps long before this witness was committed to writing, it was handed down through the generations from father to son by oral tradition. But the time came when the children of Israel under the guidance of the spirit of God committed their experiences to writing as a permanent record of God's dealing with them and for the instruction of future generations.

It is safe to say that by the first century A.D., if not earlier, the Old Testament as we have it today was accepted by the Jews as sacred scripture and distinguished from all other literature. It was written throughout in the Hebrew language, apart from a few chapters in the books of Ezra and Daniel which were written in Aramaic, a kindred language to Hebrew.

How reliable are the Old Testament sources?

Do we have the original manuscripts of the various books of the Old Testament? To this question the answer is "no." The oldest manuscript in our possession of any part of the Hebrew Bible in the original language goes back to the ninth century A.D. Quite recently portions of the Old Testament in Hebrew, including the book of Isaiah, were discovered in caves near the Dead Sea. Many of these manuscripts date back to the first century B.C. We will learn more of these finds in the near future. But the fact remains that many generations and centuries passed before the incident was recorded in manuscripts. How do we know, then, that what we find in our manuscripts is accurate? Are not mistakes bound to have arisen in the course of centuries, especially when we consider that printing was unknown and manuscripts were laboriously copied by hand?

Now while it is true that minor mistakes did arise in the copying, serious errors were unlikely for the following reasons. Detailed and meticulous instructions were given to the scribes to insure accuracy, and these men performed their tasks faithfully and with loving care. Indiscriminate copying of the Sacred Book was not allowed. The work of copying was entrusted to a section of a special tribe of Israel who were dedicated to this task. Scholars are generally agreed that the Hebrew manuscripts, as we have them, preserve the text which was in use in the first century A.D. Let us remember also that once a new manuscript had been copied and carefully checked, it was considered as authentic as its predecessor, and in many cases the older and worn manuscript was discarded. Thus we need not be unduly surprised that older manuscripts are no longer available to us.

But fortunately the Hebrew text can be checked from another source. With the victories of Alexander the Great, Greek became the common language of that day. Many Jews had left Palestine and gone to live in Egypt. In particular, large numbers of them had found a new home in Alexandria, where they learned Greek and came to use it almost as their native language. The result was a demand for the scriptures in Greek. This Greek version of the Old Testament is known as the Septuagint. The date of this translation, by seventy distinguished scholars, is the third century B.C. It was accepted as the sacred scriptures by those Jews who spoke Greek, and we know that it had a wide circulation in the East, and later in Palestine also.

13

What about the New Testament?

The New Testament was written in Greek, which was the universal language throughout the Roman Empire. Hebrew as a spoken language was dead. It was used only by the rabbis and scribes. When Christianity spread outside the borders of Palestine, it was not the Hebrew Old Testament that was used, but the Greek translation, the Septuagint. By the middle of the fourth century A.D., or perhaps even earlier, the New Testament, as we have it, had been accepted as sacred scripture. So from this time we date the acceptance of the Bible as we know it today.

What of the original Greek manuscripts of the New Testament? Here we are in a more fortunate position, for we possess two Greek manuscripts which date from the fourth century after Christ, besides fragments which go back to the second century after Christ. If you want romance, read the story of how Tischendorf discovered one of the oldest manuscripts—the famous Codex Sinaiticus—in 1844 in the monastery of St. Catherine on Mount Sinai. He managed to rescue part of it as it was about to be used to kindle a fire. Behind the record of all such discoveries one can see the hand of God at work in preserving his word through the ages for the benefit of mankind.

The Bible is put into Latin

When Greek influence lessened and the Roman Empire established itself more firmly, there came the need for a translation of the Bible in the language of the Roman Empire, which was Latin. So between 390 and 404 A.D. Jerome, the greatest biblical scholar then living, performed the rare service for the early Church of translating the entire Bible into Latin. To this translation was given

14

the name the Vulgate, which exercised a tremendous influence in the church until the Reformation.

It is interesting to note that the Vulgate remained the Bible of the Roman Church until it was superseded in 1609 by a revision, called the Douay Bible, which is now the standard and accepted translation of the Roman Catholic Church.

The Bible is put into English

With the Reformation came an entirely new attitude toward the Scriptures. Until then the knowledge of the Bible was confined to the priests, who gave the people oral instruction. The common people could not read Latin, and manuscripts were rare. But in the fifteenth century two events occurred which brought into being a revolutionary change: in 1453 the Turks captured Constantinople, and in 1454 the first printed book was given to the world. The result of the first event was that very many scholars, driven from their homes in the East, came to the West to find a haven of refuge. The language they spoke and read was Greek, which as far as western Europe was concerned was almost a dead language. Western scholars eagerly studied the literary treasures of eastern Europe brought to them by these exiled scholars. The New Testament became accessible in its original language. Along with this interest in the Greek New Testament went a like interest in the Hebrew Old Testament. This quickened interest led to a demand for the translation of the Bible in the common language of the people. The invention of the printing press helped to make this possible. A new era in the romantic story of the Bible had been opened; the Book was put into the hands of people in a language which they could read and understand.

This marks a glorious page in the history of the Bible.

The goal of the reformers was reached, but all too often it was at the price of martyrdom. Unflinchingly they bore witness to the changeless God and the unchanging gospel. When you read the story of what it cost in suffering and persecution to make the word of God available, I venture to suggest that never again will you read it without a feeling of reverence and awe.

We get the King James Version

Various translations of the Bible, or parts of it, into English were made at different periods by different men, but in the course of time the need arose for a standard translation. So it was that in 1604 King James I gave orders for a revision of the existing translations. This was methodically and systematically carried out by the leading scholars and churchmen of the day, and in 1611 the King James, or Authorized, Version of the Bible was published. This is the Bible with which the Christian Church is familiar and which has been read through these many generations. It is interesting to note that we have no record of any law passed by King or Parliament or church ordering this translation to be used. Rather it would appear that the Authorized Version won its way into the affection and regard of the common people on the basis of its own intrinsic merits. It has no rival in any literature.

The process goes on

Some three hundred years later there came an urgent desire for a new translation. But why? you ask. Because words change in meaning. New discoveries of ancient manuscripts had been made since 1611. In the light of this new knowledge it was felt that a revision would enrich and enhance the Book. The result was the publication in 1885 of the Revised Version. A few years ago scholars set to work on a new translation in the language of today. This is called the Revised Standard Version, and it is generally accepted as the most accurate translation of the Bible in modern English.

And the process will go on. Words will continue to change in meaning; new words will be coined; new discoveries will be made. No generation can lay claim to anything like a complete and final understanding of the Word of God. Who can fathom or fully understand the length and breadth and height and depth of the love of God? The Bible has borne witness through the ages to the unchanging truth of God. As we bring to bear upon it all our resources of heart and mind, we see it, not as something static, but as a living, active, dynamic force, rich with meaning and purpose for this age and all ages.

CHAPTER THREE

TESTED BY FIRE

NOW I MUST CONFESS THERE CAME A TIME WHEN MY belief in the Bible was sharply challenged. I supposed that what I had been brought up to believe about the Book was a matter of universal acceptance. The Bible was the Word of God, to be accepted without question. But I had a rude awakening. Men of great scholarship seemed to make untenable certain beliefs I held about the Book. Indeed, it was challenged in some quarters by men whose avowed intention was to discredit it entirely. I was disturbed by what is often referred to as the "critical approach." I felt that coldly intellectual men with no interest in advancing the Christian religion at all were trying to tear the Book apart and take it from me, leaving nothing but the covers.

Is the Bible true?

Many of these scholars maintained that the creation story in Genesis was utterly untenable in the light of modern science. The creation period of six days, twenty-four hours a day, was quite impossible. They seeemed to prove beyond any shadow of doubt that the evolving of the earth from the nebula, or cloud, to the time when man began to inhabit it took millions of years, if not aeons of time. They pointed out further that there were two accounts of creation which were difficult to reconcile to each other, two accounts of the flood, two accounts of the selling of Joseph into Egypt, two accounts of the founding of the monarchy, two accounts of David's introduction to King Saul, besides other parallel stories which raised the question as to which is right. The sophisticated mind, so sure of itself, asserted it was ridiculous to suppose that the upraised right arm of an old man could have any effect on the outcome of a battle or halt the processes of the universe by delaying the setting of the sun. The story of an anemic preacher tossing in the sea, swallowed by a whale in which he was domiciled three days, to be spewed up on a shore miles away to begin a preaching mission, was just too fantastic to believe. The slaughtering of children and noncombatants by the army of Israel at the command of God was too cruel and inhuman to believe. The Gospels contain so many discrepancies and contradictions about what our Lord said and did that one is at a loss to know what the facts are. It developed that the Bible has many duplications, repetitions, and inconsistencies which do not seem in order. Does God contradict himself? Scholarship asked some disturbing questions.

This approach also raised problems of another kind. I had been led to believe that the first five books of the Bible—the Pentateuch—were written by Moses. But it was pointed out that the last chapter describes in detail the death and burial of Moses. Surely he could not have written that! The book of Joshua records tht Joshua conquered the whole land of Canaan in two great military campaigns, yet Jerusalem, one of the great citadels of Canaan, did not fall until the time of David. Issues were also raised about the book of Psalms, supposed to have been written by King David; yet we find psalms that bear such titles as "A Prayer of Moses the Man of God," "For the Sons of Korah," "A Psalm of Asaph," "For Solomon."

Could David have written these? Then there is the wisdom literature which Solomon is said to have written. Yet scholars have pointed out that the language of portions of these books reveals clearly that they belong to a period centuries after the time of Solomon.

The result was that many regarded the Bible as a collection of saga and folklore, unhistorical or fictional. Indeed, it became a sign of intellectual acumen to brush aside the Book entirely. In the face of this critical approach some closed their eyes and ran away; some, cowed by this destructive criticism, tore out of the Book all the pages which did not suit their viewpoint, until the Bible looked like a village in France after bombardment; some sat back in great despair wondering what they would be compelled to surrender next.

We must face the facts

That was the situation I had to face. There the problems were. I could not deny their existence nor brush them aside. I was compelled to face them honestly. This was not a happy period. It is never easy to be shaken out of a comfortable security. The foundations of my belief seemed to be threatened by men who apparently had the facts. The old moorings were being swept aside. I was afraid that the Book was being discredited under the impact of scientific criticism.

But not for one moment in all that period did I lose my faith. I began to study and search for myself. You do not have to leave your intellect in the vestibule when you come to worship God or read the Bible. Truth need never be afraid of light. Sunlight falling on a dead log may hasten the process of decay, but sunlight falling on a living tree makes it grow and become luxuriant. Never forget that fact.

20

Let me here record what I shall refer to later, that after long, painstaking study not a single page of the Bible was discredited for me. This critical approach did not invalidate a single shred of what I believed. Indeed, I want to bear witness to the fact that through this approach I found in the Bible a God, living, active, at work in the world; a God who spoke through human beings, however imperfectly they may have spelled it out; a God who revealed himself through patriarchs, prophets, priests, and psalmists —all finite men—and finally and perfectly through Jesus Christ, his Son, our Saviour, who still speaks to us and reveals God to us by his Holy Spirit.

I met this so-called critical approach face forward, and what did I find? To my amazement and joy it has enriched the Book for me. It has not robbed me of a single scintilla of divine truth. From such an approach to the Bible we have nothing to fear. Indeed, it has made the Bible more meaningful. It has not shattered or shaken my faith in the Book; it has only deepened and strengthened it.

We owe a debt to the scholars

Let me record also how much we owe to those who have studied the Bible with painstaking scholarship. They have made a great contribution to our understanding of the purpose and nature of God. Not all these scholars by any means addressed themselves to this task with the avowed purpose of invalidating the faith we hold so dear. It is true there were those who hoped that by pointing to these so-called discrepancies they would destroy the foundations of our faith. But never forget that there were many who engaged in this critical study to make the foundations of our faith more sure. The blazing passion of their lives was a sincere search after the truth of God. We may well pause to thank God for them. They were motivated by a deep and pious desire to understand more clearly the will and mind of God. After all, God reveals himself, not so much to the clever as to the confident and trusting. Spiritual things are spiritually discerned. God has given us the resources of learning to make clear what his purposes and nature are. We are deeply indebted to these pious interpreters of revealed truth. They have made us see as never before the wisdom and the goodness of God. The more reverently and earnestly the Bible is examined and studied, the more glorious does it become. The Book has nothing to fear from such a reverent approach. Always we can say with Pastor Robinson as he prayed with the Pilgrims, kneeling on the stone pavement at Leyden, before they set sail upon their holy adventure, "God has yet greater things to reveal of himself."

CHAPTER FOUR

STANDING UNASHAMED

IN WHAT WAY HAS THIS CRITICAL APPROACH DEEPENED and enriched my faith? How has it made the Bible more meaningful to me? Let me try to answer these questions by citing from three fields of scientific investigation which have shed very considerable light on the understanding and interpretation of the Book.

Archaeology tells us more about the Book

1. In the first place, let us look at the contribution that archaeology has made to our knowledge of the Bible. This is a comparatively new field of research, the importance of which for biblical study cannot be overestimated. The subject is a fascinating one and provides us with a story which is as thrilling and romantic as a modern novel. Archaeologists are constantly making new discoveries and coming upon new finds which enable us to understand better the Bible and reconstruct its world background. Today we are in a position to trace the rise and growth of the Israelite nation and see the gradual development of its religion through the centuries against the background of the three competing world empires—Egypt, Assyria, and Babylonia.

Perhaps the best-known illustration is the story of the fall of Jericho in Josh. 6. The modern mind calls it an insult to intelligence. "And it came to pass, when the people heard the sound of the trumpet, and the people shouted with a great shout, that the wall fell down flat, so that the people went up into the city, every man straight before him, and they took the city." Whoever heard of walls falling down as the result of the blowing of trumpets and people shouting? We ask incredulously. It is easy to say that we are dealing here with nothing but a myth. But the archaeologists have shed some light on the problem. They have established that about the end of the fifteenth century before Christ or the beginning of the fourteenth century a major catastrophe overtook the ancient city of Jericho. Its main defenses comprised two parallel walls, the outer wall six feet and the inner twelve feet thick. Archaeology has also established that houses were built upon the walls themselves, the intervening space being bridged with timber. This enables us to see clearly how the harlot Rahab was able to effect the escape of the spies in Josh. 2:15 where we are told that "she let them down by a cord through the window." She was able to do this because her house was built on the city wall and gave direct access to the surrounding country.

The outer wall of the city seems to have collapsed down the slope of the hill on which Jericho was built, and this caused the inner wall to collapse also, filling the space between the walls with ruins and debris. "Traces of intense fire are plain to see, including reddened masses of brick, cracked stones, charred timbers and ashes." That is to say a part at least of the city walls tumbled down, and the city was burned with fire. What happened is that an earthquake occurred right at the very moment of the attack, and in this phenomenon the Israelites saw the hand of their God at work. Palestine, as we know, has long been subject to earthquakes.

Archaeology sheds light on a great many passages so that the Book is enriched and made to live. As the spade of the excavators turns up evidences of the life of days long gone by and the pieces gradually fall into their proper places, we can see in imagination the life of the people of those times. Real men and women—men of flesh and blood like ourselves—move across its pages. In imagination we become witnesses of historical events. We see the unfolding of a mighty historical drama, of which we feel ourselves a part. In a word the significant contribution of archaeology has been to make the Bible a living Book.

It is now possible with reasonable certainty to plot the course which the Israelites followed on their journey from Egypt to Mount Sinai and from Mount Sinai to the Promised Land, to reconstruct the scenes portrayed in the book of Joshua, to pinpoint the dramatic episodes in the life of the Hebrew people. Through archaeology we can walk, at least in imagination, with our Lord along the highways and byways of Palestine, through its towns and villages, from the winding road to the manger, to the Via Dolorosa, to Calvary. Incidents in the life of Jesus from his birth in Bethlehem through his boyhood in Nazareth, and later on during the three years of his earthly ministry in various parts of Palestine, to his death on the cross, have been made more certain. Next to a visit to the Holy Land itself —an invaluable experience for any student of the Bible —there is nothing I know which will give you such a vivid picture of the background to the Book as a study of the results of archaeological research in recent years. Thanks to archaeology we realize as we make our way through the pages of the Bible that here we are standing on holy ground; here we are treading where the saints have trod.

Students of history enrich our knowledge

2. The second field of scientific investigation which has enriched the Bible is historical research. It is now possible

to see the history of the Israelites and their religious development within the framework of world history. We can also see the influence which this comparatively insignificant people exercised upon the cultures of the surrounding nations and subsequently upon the whole world. Today we know a great deal about the language in which the books of the Bible were written. We know the circumstances which produced them. We know the period of history out of which the books of the Bible came and the men who wrote them. Against this background of greatly increased knowledge we see the Bible in time and beyond time.

One important result of historical research is the new and more accurate setting it provides for the prophets of Israel. They speak in the name of God to the needs of their own day and generation. That is the great miracle of the Old Testament—the prophetic consciousness. The prophets, though fallible human beings, were so sensitive in spirit and so deeply consecrated to the service of God that they were able to discern his will and purpose. God did not override human personality; he used it. He spoke to the ages through men who were after all frail and human. What a light this interpretation casts upon the significance and importance of God-called men! The God who in times past made use of finite men as the vehicles of his divine revelation, as interpreters of his will and purpose, can and does still act in like manner today.

As an illustration of all this take the second half of the book of Isaiah, beginning at chapter 40. What is the background of these chapters? It is the meteoric rise to fame of Cyrus, the Persian king. The prophet, whose name is unknown to us, watched the victories of Cyrus and reached the conviction that God was behind Cyrus, who was his chosen instrument for the fulfillment of his purposes. This conviction fired the prophet with the hope that Cyrus would set them free and permit them to return to their own land—a hope which was in fact fulfilled. The background of these chapters is unquestionably the exile in Babylon and the imminent prospect of a return home. Against an exilic background these chapters throb with hope and expectancy. Is it any wonder, then, that in our times of doubt and despair which so strangely parallel that era, we turn to this prophet again and again? For here the note of faith and certainty is struck in no uncertain sound. To a people who had lost heart and hope, who despaired of the possibility that the mighty Babylonian Empire could be overthrown, there came a voice which had in it the note of eternity, "All flesh is grass . . . . The grass withereth, the flower fadeth: but the word of our God shall stand for ever."

Or think of another illustration of this historical insight: the letters of Paul in the New Testament. These letters arose out of specific needs, problems, and crises which had arisen in the early church. Sometimes it was a personal letter; sometimes it was a circular letter dealing with specific problems which confronted the group. Upon these perplexities the great apostle brought the wisdom and light of God. So once again in the New Testament as in the Old Testament we see the interplay of divine and human factors clarified for us in historical research. It has helped to make clear the relevance of the Word of God, not only for that age, but for every age.

Students of languages shed light on the Book

3. In the third place, our knowledge of the actual Hebrew and Greek texts of the Bible has been greatly enriched by scholars who devoted their lives to a study of these and kindred languages. It is impossible to overesti-

mate the new light which has been shed on many passages in the Bible by the scientific study of sentence structure, phraseology, and even of individual words. It means a great deal to know that the text of the Bible which we use is accurate and exact. It is in this field that scholars have made a real contribution to our understanding of the Book. New texts in new and hitherto unknown languages are constantly being discovered. These finds illumine for us passages which have been obscure and difficult both to understand and to translate.

Further, we all know how words often change in meaning with the passing of time. Thought forms and expressions which were common in previous generations are no longer in use in our time. The King James Version was written in seventeenth-century English, but many of its words and phrases are outmoded and obsolete. Biblical scholarship has reverently and prayerfully set itself to this task. It is making more meaningful the Word of God that it may speak with more telling power to the hearts and consciences of men today.

But let me not be misunderstood. I was brought up on the King James Version of the Bible. Portions of it I learned by heart, and these I can never forget. I love its stately beauty, the grandeur and the majesty of its language. For me no other translation can ever have quite the same appeal. But there are portions in which the meaning is far from clear. And we cannot disregard the new light which God in his wisdom is continually bestowing upon us through new discoveries and new knowledge.

Let me illustrate by referring to N. H. Snaith's book *The Distinctive Ideas of the Old Testament*. In a very well-known passage in Isa. 40 we read in the King James Version, "The voice said, Cry. And he said, What shall I cry? All flesh is grass, and all the goodliness thereof is as the flower of the field." The difficulty here is that the Hebrew word translated "goodliness" occurs nowhere else in the Old Testament with this meaning. The Hebrew word means "steadfast faithfulness" or perhaps "firmness." The reference, therefore, is not to the beauty of wild flowers but to their frailty. Man, the prophet says, is like the grass and the wild flowers—here today and gone tomorrow. The emphasis is on the transitoriness of all human life and human achievements. By way of contrast the word of God is firm, steadfast, and enduring.

Or again, in Isa. 41:14 we read as follows, "Fear not, thou worm Jacob, and ye men of Israel." Scholars have long felt that the translation "men of Israel" was incorrect as it does not provide a parallel to "thou worm Jacob." But this could not be proved. Now, however, it has been clearly demonstrated that the Hebrew word translated "men" comes from an Accadian root which means "louse." The correct translation, then, is "Thou worm Jacob, and ye lice of Israel"—a translation which gives the necessary parallelism and indicates the insignificance of both Jacob and Israel. And so in many cases. New knowledge, of which past generations were quite unaware, has enabled us to interpret the Word of God more faithfully and more accurately. This is a matter not of boasting but of humble gratitude to Almighty God.

This is equally true of the Greek New Testament. Thanks to new discoveries we have acquired new knowledge of the meaning of Greek words and phrases. In I Pet. 1:7 we read in the King James Version, "That the trial of your faith, being much more precious than of gold that perisheth, though it be tried with fire, might be found unto praise and honour and glory at the appearing of Jesus Christ." Only recently have we come to learn that the Greek word here translated "trial" does not have this meaning at all. It means "genuine part," or "genuineness" —a meaning which alters the sense of the passage and makes it live for us.

Adolf Deissmann in *Light from the Ancient East* reminds us that when Jesus sent forth his disciples to preach, he said according to Matt. 10:8-10, "Freely ye have received, freely give. Provide neither gold, nor silver, nor brass in your purses, Nor scrip for your journey." But what does scrip mean here? Most people have assumed that it means a traveling bag or a bread bag, both of which suit the context. But another meaning has been suggested by an inscription on one of the monuments—the beggar's collecting bag. The meaning, then, is that the apostles are not to take money with them, nor are they to beg.

Let us use all the God-given helps we have

So we see how modern scholarship has enriched our knowledge of the Book and removed many difficulties. It is true, of course, that scholarship by itself cannot show us the heart of this Book of books. Nor is piety by itself adequate to interpret it. Both are necessary. Let us bring to the study of the Bible complete frankness and honesty. Let us openly admit the problems with which it confronts us, without trying to gloss them over. Let us come with open minds and eager hearts. Let us make use of all the God-given helps we have—all the resources of modern biblical scholarship. Then for us too the Bible will become alive, and we will see it as God's living word for our day and generation.

Tried in the fires of criticism, as no other book in the history of the world has ever been tried, the Bible has emerged victorious, richer, and more meaningful than ever. The Christian faith rests upon sure and solid foundations. The Book has stood the test of critical analysis.

CHAPTER FIVE

WHERE GOD AND MAN MEET

MANY TIMES I HAVE BEEN ASKED, "WHY DO WE NEED the Bible?" If we can find our way to God directly through prayer and worship, what is the necessity for this Book? What purpose does it fulfill? Having accepted its authenticity and knowing something of its content, the question arises, What are we to do with it? Why have we given it the position of priority above all other religious writings? In other words, what is the underlying importance and aim of the Book?

In order to answer that question intelligently and honestly, I must begin by saying that there is in the heart of man an ageless, nameless, indefinable longing for someone beyond himself. Deep in the human heart there is a desire for fellowship with God. We are conscious of being separated from one for whose companionship we long and whose forgiveness we seek. Man cannot live by bread alone. There is something in him which calls out continuously, "Oh that I knew where I might find him!" It is eternally true, "Our hearts are restless till they rest in thee."

Underneath this topsy-turvy world, tumbling apart into broken and brittle bits, full of disintegration, there is the longing for something that can give it stability and hold it together. We have a way of saying that this is a new world and that hitherto undreamed forces are at work. But in reality this is the same old world as it has always been, surging with the element of change and decay. Civilization is always changing. We may talk about a new culture, a new science, or a new economics, but there is always at work in this world the same ageless process of change and decay. The human heart surges with the same old hopes, the same dreams, the same sorrows, and the same ageless longing. To this ageless yearning in a changing world comes the message of a timeless book.

The Bible is man's highway to God

The Bible seems to gather up and express for mankind this ageless groping for someone beyond himself. It expresses as no other book in all the world has done this longing of the human heart for God. You meet it in the Greeks, who came saying, "Sir, we would see Jesus." Paul found it in Athens when he pointed the people of the city to the altar to the unknown God which stood in their midst. There are times when with Nicodemus of old we call out, "How can these things be?" Philip in his anguish of soul exclaimed, "Shew us the Father, and it sufficeth."

We are conscious of a relationship which has been broken and which must be re-established. We are dissatisfied with what we are and where we are. Our whole secular world today, conscious of its material power, still repeats the plaintive and poignant inquiry of the rich young ruler, "What lack I yet?" You hear Peter saying, "Depart from me; for I am a sinful man, O Lord." The thief on the cross calls out, "Remember me when thou comest into thy kingdom." In the heart of things there is a search for a depth so deep and a height so inaccessible that nothing can disturb it. It is a well-known fact that there is not anywhere and never has been a city without its altar or a nation without its temple. In our better moments we become aware of the truth, "Against thee, thee only, have I sinned."

While one comes upon this longing in almost every page of the Book, it is in the Psalms, and especially in the book of Job, that all this frustration and search come to focus.

The book of Psalms is a mirror of the ages. Here we witness a panorama of the religious life of the Jewish people. We are given glimpses into the innermost recesses of their souls. We come upon the outpouring of the human heart to God in prayer and supplication, in praise and thanksgiving, in anguish over sin and deep penitence of heart, in pain and despair. Sometimes the individual speaks, sometimes the nation. Hope and despair are strangely intermingled—hope in the power and the might of God, despair over the injustice in the world and man's inhumanity to man. We see hands outstretched to God, groping in the darkness for the assurance of his presence. Here too we find the joyful experience of forgiveness. What we have in the Psalms, therefore, is a cross section of Jewish life—home and family life, private and community life—all searching, groping, yearning for God. The psalms spring from these deep needs.

In the hour of guilt man lifts the prayer: "Create in me a clean heart, O God." In the hour of aspiration he calls out, "My soul waiteth for the Lord more than they that watch for the morning." All his groping and frustration are resolved in, "I shall be satisfied, when I awake, with thy likeness." "Lead me to the rock that is higher than I." The hopes and fears of all the years come to focus in the Psalter. In the mirror of the psalms we see ourselves reflected—our hopes and fears, our longings and aspirations, our problems and our pain, our anguish and our dilemmas. The outpouring of the psalmists' hearts speaks to our own hearts and for our own hearts. That is why the Psalter is so meaningful for public and private worship; it has no parallel in the devotional literature of the world.

You meet this same groping after God in the book of Job. It is the epic of a human soul struggling to find God. It is the story of a man who is stripped of his wealth, family, and possessions crying out in the night for someone who can tell him the meaning of these things. It does not answer the question of suffering, but it does give an answer to the question of how to deal with it. Through the long night of pain, misunderstanding, and adversity Job came to find an answer in the assurance, "I know that my redeemer liveth." The Bible is, therefore, a highway up which man travels to God.

The Bible is God's highway to man

But the Bible is more than a search of man for God and a highway up which man travels to the home of his soul. Let me say ever so clearly so that no one need ever doubt: The Bible is a book about God. Indeed, it would be more accurate to say that the Bible is the Word of God. Through this Book, God has spoken and speaks to the longing of the human heart. It is a record not simply of man's search for God but of God's search for man. The Bible is primarily not the record of the history of a chosen people, but rather the record of God's revealing of himself to man through the centuries. It is not enough to stretch up one's hand to heaven and cry imploringly, "Oh that I knew where I might find him!" What we want to know is: Is there a hand which reaches down to us? The Bible does not leave one in the dark very long on that issue. If we may think of it as a road up which man travels to God, it is even more true to say that it is a highway down which God travels to meet man.

The Bible is, therefore, a book about God. It is not a book about science. In some respects, indeed, the Bible is a very unscientific book. I am glad that it is so. If it were a book of science, it would soon be outdated and would have to be rewritten every generation. It is not a book about science, although it has much scientific data. It is not a book about botany, although it has some lovely things to say about flowers. It is not a book on astronomy, although it tells us much about stars. It is not a book of jurisprudence, although law is there. If you want to know what stands at the center of it, you must read again:

> "If with all your heart ye truly seek me,
> Ye shall ever surely find me."
> Thus saith our God.

The Bible does not tell us how to make machinery, but it does tell us how to make men who are safe with machines. It does not tell us how to build political techniques, but it does tell us how to make men who can be trusted with government. It does not tell us how to build roads, but it does tell us how to make men who can be trusted on these roads. It is a book about God. It gives courage to the timid, companionship to the lonely, confidence to the confused, and forgiveness to the sinful. God has made himself known to mankind through his Word.

The God who wrote his omnipotence on star clusters and milky ways, who wrote his painstaking care in the making of the simplest crustacean cells, also wrote his endless mercy and compassion across the pages of this Book of books. In it humanity, sobbing out its defeat by sin, finds a matchless triumph through divine deliverance. Its pages are radiant with everlasting hope and resonant with the voice of the Redeemer. What a compass is to a pilot, what a song is to a weary heart, and what a latch is to a homeless wanderer, the Bible is to us.

I am well aware that all this, which I believe and hold precious, raises certain questions. Is it possible for God to make himself known to man? Can the finite grasp the infinite? Can finite man define in human terms the reality which is God? Are human words big enough to hold divine truth?

To these and all similar questions the answer of the Bible is clear. By the use of his own unaided powers man could never come to a knowledge of God. You cannot deduce God from already known facts. Man knows God only because God has chosen to reveal himself to man. And man's capacity to know God is itself a gift from God.

How does this process of revelation work? How did God reveal himself to man? Through human instruments. For all his imperfections man, made in the image of God, has communicated God to man, however difficult it may be to explain or analyze. The fact stands that God has revealed himself to man.

Let me illustrate this in two very simple ways. The first is this: One day you go to your record player to play an old favorite song of some great artist. You have not heard that song for a long time, nor have you used the record player. You discover that the needle is poor, the connections are loose, the record is warped, and yet you recognize the voice. It is unmistakable. So it is in this Book. For all of his failings and shortcomings man, made in the image of God, has been able to understand him and say with Kepler, "I think Thy thoughts after Thee, O God." There have been men through the long centuries who have walked so close to God and have been lifted so near to him that they saw what nobody else saw, heard what nobody else heard, and felt what nobody else felt. What they saw, heard, and felt, they wrote down and transmitted to the ages.

The second is this: If we look at the light of the sun directly or through plain glass, it is without color. But if we see it through a stained-glass window, it is modified by the medium through which it passes. It takes on the varied colorings of the stained-glass window. In like manner the revelation of God, while it comes directly from him, reflects the human instruments which he uses. The truth that comes from him is affected by the channels through which it comes. It is seen by human eyes and interpreted by human minds. Thus the perfect truth of God is not seen by imperfect man. But some light filters through; some truth is manifest. And all light that has its source in God is enduring light; all truth that comes from him is eternal truth.[1] This is the great glory of the Bible; this is its purpose—it serves to reveal God.

It is possible, therefore, for finite man to grasp, at least in some measure, the infinite God. There were men who saw God, who heard his voice and felt his presence, who lived so intimately with him that they became channels of the divine communication. That is the meaning of the phrase which occurs so often in the Old Testament—"The word of the Lord came." It came to the patriarchs, to Moses, to Joshua, to Amos, to Hosea, to Isaiah, to Jeremiah, to Ezekiel, to Haggai, to Zechariah, to Joel. These men lived close to God and were in tune with him. They saw so much more clearly the heart and mind and will and purpose of God that their words became charged with the very authority of God himself. They were certain that God was speaking in them and through them.

You remember the story of the child Samuel. Three

[1] I owe this illustration to H. H. Rowley, *The Rediscovery of the Old Testament* (Westminster).

37

times one night while he was asleep in the temple he heard a voice calling him by name, "Samuel, Samuel." Three times he rose from his couch in answer to the voice and ran to the aged priest Eli to ask why he had called him. Twice Eli denied that he had spoken his name. But when Samuel appeared the third time, Eli knew who it was who had summoned the youth. "Go, lie down," he told Samuel: "and it shall be, if he call thee, that thou shalt say, Speak, Lord; for thy servant heareth." So the infinite God makes himself known to finite men.

Let me further illustrate. Take Amos, for example, who was the first of the prophets to set down his message in writing. He was a shepherd and a tender of sycamore trees. One day as he was going about his ordinary tasks, God spoke to him and said, "Go, prophesy unto my people Israel." The story as Amos tells it is as plain and simple as that. But what was he to prophesy? What message was he to proclaim as God's spokesman?

The time was about 750 B.C. Outwardly Israel was enjoying a period of prosperity such as she had not known since Solomon. Trade flourished, and wealth poured into the treasuries of the rich. But side by side with this great wealth went extreme poverty. To a large extent the land was owned by the rich, who had great estates. These estates were run on a system of forced slave labor, and the agricultural workers were little better than serfs. The people had little means of redress as the law courts were controlled by the rich. Justice everywhere was perverted. Money could buy a verdict anywhere.

Religion too had lost its meaning. The priests at the shrines worked hand in hand with the rich. Only outwardly was religion flourishing. The altars smoked from morning till night with sacrifices. All the religious ritual was punctiliously observed. But underneath all this cold formalism there was smoldering a deep resentment. Did God really demand all these elaborate sacrifices while hunger and starvation were rife among the people? It was all very well for the wealthy to pride themselves upon the observance of all these costly sacrifices, but what of the poor who could not afford them? Such were the conditions which prevailed when Amos appeared on the scene to speak for God.

He was not unprepared for the task to which God had called him. His life as a shepherd in the wilderness of Judea was a hard one and a dangerous one. It was a constant battle against wild beasts and the elemental forces of nature. In the silent and solitude of the desert Amos meditated long on the nature and character of God and his will for his people. Then suddenly the light dawned upon his soul, and Amos looked into the heart of God. That was something new and hitherto unknown. So through Amos as his instrument God made himself known in terms of righteousness to his people and through them to the ages. The words were the words of Amos; the message was a message from God.

As with Amos, so it was with all the prophets. Step by step, as men were able to comprehend him, God unfolded his nature and his character, his plan and purpose, through finite man. Each prophet sheds some new light on the character of God, lifting the veil so that man might know him, at least in part.

Jesus is the Bible's fullest revelation

But the final and complete revelation of God in the Bible is in Jesus Christ. It could never be through words. Language always breaks down in the attempt to describe or define the infinite. Words are not big enough. The finite can never hold the infinite. So it came to pass that in the fullness of time God sent His Son, and "the Word was made flesh, and dwelt among us, . . . full of grace and truth."

When men saw Jesus, they called out, "Emmanuel, . . . God with us." He is the Word incarnate. In Christ you have God's final revelation of himself. The unknown writer of the book of Hebrews begins, "God, who at sundry times and in divers manners spake in time past unto the fathers by the prophets, hath in these last days spoken unto us by his Son." This is what the Christian Church through all the ages has meant by revelation.

When you ask, therefore, what is the purpose of the Bible, you have the answer in the last sentence of the twentieth chapter of the last book of the New Testament perhaps to have been written: "These are written, that ye might believe that Jesus is the Christ, the Son of God; and that believing ye might have life through his name."

CHAPTER SIX

THE DRAMA UNFOLDS

MUCH OF WHAT I HAVE WRITTEN SO FAR IS PERHAPS quite familiar to many, and yet there is everywhere a strange ignorance of the content of the Book. We know a good deal about the Bible, but we do not know the Bible. What, then, is this Bible?

The Bible is not a book but a library

To begin with, it is well to bear in mind that the Bible is not a book but a library. It is made up of sixty-six different books: thirty-nine in the Old Testament and twenty-seven in the New Testament. It was not written at one sitting and so tossed off into history. Mark Twain once said that "a Bible like that would be chloroform in print." The Bible was written by some forty people over a period of fifteen hundred years in an area equal to that which lies between the Atlantic seaboard and the Rocky Mountains.

The Bible was written by different kinds of people. Among these writers there were a shepherd, a physician, a king, a farmer, a historian, a poet, a fisherman, a priest, a lawyer, and a philosopher. It was written by different men with different dilemmas. Each tried to meet some one problem that was foremost in the minds of the people for whom he wrote. Each wrote independently of the others.

You have, therefore, in the Bible two thousand years of

41

changing life, yet the Book does not change. It is against the background of an ever-changing world, with its new and yet ever-old problems and needs, that the Bible is set. Only so can it be rightly understood. The Bible speaks to human life in all its many and varying aspects: in the home and in the community, in the nation and in the world, in peace and in war, in joy and in suffering, in youth and in age, in victory and in defeat. And over all these it sheds the light of God's unchanging purpose. Thus it gives to all human life a meaning and a goal.

Because it was written by so many different kinds of people, it is at home in the cottage and in the palace, in hospitals and in prisons, in cathedrals and at firesides. When people read the Bible, they should go to it as they go to a library. Sometimes they will be in the mood for poetry; then they turn to the Psalms. Sometimes they feel in the mood for romance, and they will come upon the incomparable love story of Ruth and Esther. Sometimes they are historically minded, and then the books of Judges and of the Kings open before them. Sometimes they feel the need of some quickening impact upon the conscience; then the books of the Law become most helpful. There are times when they wonder what life and the universe are all about; then it is that the sense of purpose and the destiny of life will be clarified in the rich imagery and the revelations of the prophets and of the apostle John. When people use the Bible in some such fashion, they will never become wearied of it but will have a longing for it.

You do not have to be a scholar to understand the Bible. It is so simple that "he who runs may read" and a little child can understand it. Just as man raised corn and wheat without knowing the chemical properties of the soil which brought his harvests or the significance of soil fertilization, but simply lived by the rewards of the harvest, so men have fed their souls on this bread of life without any knowledge of its structure or the technique by which it was written. We can say with Coleridge: "It finds me," and with Sir Walter Scott, sitting in his armchair in his library at Abbotsford: "There is no other book now; it is the Bible."

What is the Bible about?

Now let us examine that Bible more closely. The revelation of God of which I have spoken is set in time, in the history and experience of a people. The book of Genesis is the book of beginnings: the beginning of the earth from a cloud drifting through space to the forming of the world which man inhabits, the beginning of family life, the beginning of sin and transgression, the beginning of worship, the beginning of patriarchal life, and the emergence of the Hebrew race, concluding with the sojourn in Egypt.

The story moves on in Exodus to the oppression which the Hebrew people suffered in Egypt, where they made bricks without straw. At last they broke the chains of bondage under the inspired leadership of Moses and crossed the Red Sea by divine intervention. So began the long, lonely, forty years of wandering through the uncharted wastes of the desert. They halted at Mount Sinai, where the covenant relationship was established, the decalogue promulgated, and the tabernacle was set up, bearing witness to God's gracious and constant presence in their midst.

In Leviticus you have the record of the laws and regulations which guided them in their desert wanderings and ultimately brought them a sense of unity. The book of Numbers records the growing sense of solidarity, the census, and further episodes. In Deuteronomy we find a recapitulation of past history, followed by a second series of laws, dealing with every phase of life: economic, social, political, and religious. It contains also the superb final address of Moses to the children of Israel before he climbed Mount Pisgah, where God took him.

Joshua is the heroic tale of the armies of Israel conquering the land of Canaan and how it came to be divided among the twelve tribes. Joshua was their leader in this difficult task of national unity. In Judges you have the account of the first attempts of the nation to organize itself through leadership which God provided for them in periods of emergency. Here you meet the colorful personalities of Deborah, Gideon, Samson, and Samuel. Then follows the organization and establishment of the nation under kings, beginning with Saul and reaching its zenith in David and Solomon. Then comes the twilight as the nation falls apart into two kingdoms, each ending in exile and captivity. In the midst of this account of the unfolding of the nation with all its glory and tragedy, one comes upon the moving story of Ruth. That tale stands like an oasis in a desert. During these long years of growth and later disintegration you meet this rare company of poets who turned the hearts of the people to God through the incomparable Psalmody.

In the fearful hours of impending doom and judgment, when the nation was falling apart, God raised up the prophets, who warned the nation of the perilous road it was traveling. They also held before the people the divine assurance, when they were scattered, that they would one day return to rebuild the waste places if only they would repent. The first of these prophets was Amos with his insistence upon justice, followed by Hosea and that undaunted, fearless company of God-inspired men including Isaiah, Jeremiah, and Ezekiel, and those often referred to as the minor prophets.

44

God fulfilled his promise, the nation repented, and they returned to rebuild the waste places of Canaan. The story of that period of rebuilding you will find in the books of Ezra and Nehemiah. As the account of the building of the nation is lit up with the story of Ruth, so this period of strain and struggle is brightened with the romantic tale of Esther.

The bitter experiences of exile and the tragic story of nationl disintegration forced the ancient people to consider what was the meaning of these events. With that question they grappled in the book of Job, which contains the assurance, "I know that my Redeemer liveth." In the period of rebuilding the Hebrews became aware also of those moral standards and patterns of conduct in which alone they would fine security and peace. That is the significance of what is often referred to as the wisdom literature: Ecclesiastes, Poverbs, and the Song of Solomon.

During all these generations of stress and turmoil the Hebrew people never lost the assurance that one day the lost glory would return to them. They held fast to the firm conviction that the rule of God and his kingdom would yet be established. On that note of undying hope the Old Testament closes.

Then the New Testament opens, and the ancient prophecy is fulfilled. Christ walks among men, full of grace and truth—the final, complete, and satisfying revelation of God.

As you look back upon the story, one is impressed with the gradual unfolding and ever-changing revelation of God through men who were divinely guided. God opens the windows to let in as much light as man can endure at the moment. If more were given, it would only blind him. God reveals himself to man only as he is able to apprehend. Thus in the Bible we have a progressive unfolding of God. And by this I mean that there are different levels of spiritual experience. There is a growth in man's conception of God. Let me trace some of these unfoldings with you.

We see the unfolding revelation of God

When the Book opens, you meet him as Creator of the earth and all that is in it. But what was their conception of this Creator? They thought of him as one walking in the garden and talking with man. Then the veil is lifted upon their understanding, and they thought of him as a tribal deity. Later you meet a further unfolding, and he is conceived of as the national god of the Hebrew people. In the period of the conquest and the establishment of the kingdom he is portrayed primarily as a war God, fighting in behalf of his chosen people.

With the coming of the prophets the conception of God becomes spiritual and moral. In the desert Amos experiences a fresh unfolding: "Let judgment run down as waters, and righteousness as a mighty stream." In the tragic experience of a broken home Hosea saw God as one of lovingkindness. Isaiah caught the further vision of God and wrote: "Holy, holy, holy, is the Lord of hosts." In exile the Hebrew people hanged their harps upon the willows and wept when they remembered Zion. They supposed that in leaving the frontiers of their country they had left their God behind. They thought of him as having a zonal influence beyond which he could not function. But in the second half of Isaiah you have the revelation of God without national frontiers—one who embraces in his concern all people and all races of mankind.

Then the New Testament opens, and in Jesus you have the final and all-glorious revealing of God: a God whose

46

children we all are, who forgives, who redeems, who holds us with a love that will not let us go, who suffers with us and for us.

We see the unfolding idea of sin

Notice also the unfolding idea of sin in the Bible and a growing moral consciousness. You will meet the idea of sin upon different levels. In its early pages sin is regarded as a violation of tribal custom, tradition, and family practice. Sin is taboo. There was no great emphasis on sin in terms of individual transgression and personal responsibility. But when you come to the prophets, you meet a more profound conception. They regarded sin as a violation of the law of a righteous God, bringing individual retribution and judgment. But in the New Testament you see what sin really is. It stands unmasked in all its dreadful nature and consequences. Calvary lays bare the extreme to which sin will go to have its way. It is something more than a violation of tradition or the command of a righteous God. It is the denial of the God of love.

We see the unfolding idea of sacrifice

It is interesting also to trace the unfolding idea of sacrifice. The Book opens with an altar upon which men placed the fruit of the ground and the firstlings of the flock. You even meet in its early stages evidences of human sacrifice as when Abraham went out to offer his son, Isaac, and God stayed his hand. But in the prophets you see a much higher and holier conception of sacrifice. It is not a matter of the observance of external customs and rites, but an inward yielding of heart to the will of God. "The sacrifices of God are a broken spirit: a broken and a contrite heart, O God, thou wilt not despise."

Then in the New Testament you meet Christ, who is

47

our eternal sacrifice, offered once and for all for the remission of our sins. It is a matter of not what man has done for God but what God has done for man. Calvary is the final revealing of the love of God in giving his Son to be the propitiation for our sins. The Cross is the full and sufficient sacrifice. "Behold the Lamb of God, which taketh away the sin of the world."

We see the unfolding idea of immortality

So also you can trace the unfolding idea of immortality. There are portions in the Old Testament which leave one wondering if faith in another life is justified. Take the book of Ecclesiastes: "The living know that they shall die." "That which befalleth the sons of men befalleth beasts; even one thing befalleth them: as the one dieth, so dieth the other; yea, they have all one breath; so that a man hath no preeminence above a beast." That is not a very exalted or comforting word.

But then you turn the pages of the Book to the New Testament, and you come upon that all-glorious assurance, "Now is Christ risen from the dead, and become the firstfruits of them that slept." "As in Adam all die, even so in Christ shall all be made alive."

Man's understanding changes

When once you grasp the significance of an unfolding revelation, the apparent inconsistencies of the Bible no longer exist. God does not change. He is the same yesterday, today, and forever. But man's understanding of God changes. We grow in grace and knowledge. The nature of God and his purpose for man enlarge and deepen with every fresh apprehension. It is for this reason that you see light and truth on different levels. When, therefore, you come upon some conception of life or religion which seems untenable today, you must always ask yourself upon what level of unfolding does it stand. Not that they are false, but imperfect; not that they are untrue, but incomplete. That was the meaning of Jesus when he said, "Ye have heard that it hath been said by them of old time, . . . But I say unto you . . ." We know that Christ is the final revealing of God, and therefore nothing below the standard of Jesus is binding upon us.

One need not be afraid of this approach to the Bible. It will deepen your affection for it and enrich your understanding of it. Let me repeat here again: God does not change—only man's understanding of God changes in the light of fuller revelation.

The Bible is our rule and guide

We speak of the Bible as history, poetry, biography, and philosophy. But it is much more than the sum total of all these. It is, of course, a book of history with its searching judgments of the nations, and more especially of the Hebrew people, whom God set apart as his chosen. It is quite correct to say that it is a book of morals. Never will a civilization survive or a nation long endure which disregards the Ten Commandments, the Sermon on the Mount, and the Golden Rule. We readily acknowledge that it is a book of poetry than which nothing finer has been penned by man. No finer drama will ever be written than that of Job. It is true there is romance in the Bible; you will not find anywhere in the whole sweep of literature a more poignant love story than that of Ruth. There is also biography with the delicate and discerning character delineations of Joseph and Moses, Paul and Peter. The Bible also contains collections of correspondence. You will find twenty letters crowded together in the New Testament, thirteen of which are by one writer. And these letters have no parallel anywhere.

And yet the Bible is more than all these. It is a record of man's growing experience of God and of God's revelation of himself to man. It satisfies because it answers the questions: Does it bring God nearer? Does it call out the angels of our better selves? Does it provide a way out of sin and frustration? Is it a lamp to the darkened, a comfort to the saddened, an anchor to the storm-tossed, a compass to those who have lost their way? Does this Book bring peace, joy, and strength? The unfailing answer to all these questions is always and everywhere, "Yes, a thousand times, yes."

The Christian religion is not the only religion built upon a book. Many religions of the earth, dead and living, have had their sacred literature, but how pitifully unavailing they are in the quest for peace and satisfaction! The Egyptian religion has had its forty-five sacred books. Only one is extant today, and that deals with burial ceremonies and magic. Brahminism has its Upanishads, but they only hold terror and fear before their readers. Buddhism has its Tripitaka of three thousand volumes which only the wealthy and affluent can afford to own and read. Confucianism has its sacred writings, but they deal only with etiquette and manners. Islam has its Koran, but its language is provincial, its ethics are depressing, its paradise is carnal, and its God is kismet.

But to the Christian believer the Bible is the only rule and guide of faith and practice. It lifts his horizons, deepens his sense of compassion, quickens his sense of guilt, assures him of a redeeming grace, enables him to live with a steadying purity, and provides him with an unfaltering faith in an unfailing God—whose ways, though past finding out, are altogether ways of love.

CHAPTER SEVEN

IT COMES TO FOCUS

THE NEW TESTAMENT WITH ITS TWENTY-SEVEN BOOKS opens with the four Gospels. We do not have a biography of Jesus. What might be called "A Life of Christ" does not exist. We do not have anything to parallel what is often referred to as biography. So much of his life is a closed book. There are vast areas of which we know nothing and which will forever remain hidden.

The four Gospels are unique and different. One Gospel begins with his public ministry. Another Gospel opens with his baptism in the River Jordan. Only Luke records the detailed story of his birth, while Matthew traces his genealogy through David to Abraham and records only the visit of the wise men. There is only one incident recorded of his boyhood life: his visit to the Temple at the age of twelve. There are many silent years, while one third of each Gospel deals with the last week of his life.

The Gospels give us a "witness" of Jesus

It is well to remember that the Gospel writers did not pretend to give the story of his life; that was least in their thinking. They were not concerned about giving a detailed account of every episode and incident from his birth to his death. They were interested only in telling the effect which Jesus had upon them. They wrote about those things in his ministry which impressed them most and which they believed most vital. They put into writing the experiences which influenced them most deeply. Indeed, for many years they made no effort to reduce their experiences to writing.

It never occurred to them to write a long treatise of who he was and what he was. They simply went about bearing witness to what Christ had come to mean to them and what events in his life impressed them most. Their testimony was, "One thing I know, that, whereas I was blind, now I see." "That . . . which we have heard, which we have seen with our eyes, which we have looked upon, and our hands have handled: . . . that which we have seen and heard declare we unto you." They felt duty bound to tell the story, but it never occurred to them to write it.

Another reason why they did not reduce their witness to writing was because they believed in the imminent return of Jesus. They were convinced he would come back again soon. But as the years passed and he did not return, and while they themselves were growing older, they determined to put in writing what they had preached. It seems to be almost by chance that we have any record of him at all. It makes you hold your breath and shudder to think how casually it came into being. If ever you need any proof of the authenticity and genuineness of the Gospels, you will find it in that fact. God had a hand in it, guiding men, perhaps without their knowledge. Herein you have the evidence of the inspiration of the Book.

What we have, therefore, is not a biography but a testament or witness. We do not have a narrative, but a sketch; not a photograph, but a portrait. The four Gospels were written by four men, each approaching the life of Christ from his own point of view. Each records some things which are peculiar to it and some things common to all. There is contrast in these Gospels, but not contradiction.

The first three Gospels have much in common and are quite distinct from the Fourth Gospel. The first three Gospels describe the active ministry of Jesus; the Fourth Gospel deals with the inner life of Jesus. We may liken them to a picture of the physical world. The first three give you pictures of glorious bits of landscape; the fourth looks upon it from above and floods it with light. In the early Christian tradition these four Gospels had distinct symbols. Matthew is described in the symbol of a man, Mark in the symbol of a lion, Luke in the symbol of an ox, John in the symbol of an eagle.

Matthew speaks to the Jews

The Gospel of Matthew was not the first to be written, but it rightfully and logically should be placed first. It is based upon a collection of memories or notes which Matthew had recorded and were later edited into our present Gospel. It was either an expression of how the Jewish Christians thought of Jesus or a witness to the Jewish world by a disciple of the significance of Jesus. Because the Gospel was clearly an appeal to the Jewish community, it constantly links Jesus to the Old Testament. His ancestry is traced back to the house of David and Abraham. The first two chapters record five incidents proving how Jesus fulfilled ancient prophecy. He stands recorded as Messiah, Lawgiver, King. The Gospel of Matthew links Jesus to the past.

Mark shows us the strong Son of God

The Gospel of Mark, though it stands second in the New Testament, was actually the first Gospel to be written down. Indeed much of Matthew and Luke was copied from Mark. Mark was the companion of Peter when he preached in Rome. He carefully treasured and wrote down what Peter told him and the people about Jesus. All that would appeal to the Romans, who worshiped power and action. The stories are vividly told. They have about them a dash and color. Christ stands revealed as the strong Son of God. It is not interested in linking Jesus to the past or future. It emphasizes what he can do in the present.

Luke shows us the tenderness of Jesus

The third Gospel was written by Luke, the only non-Jew to write a Gospel. He was a Greek, well educated, who wrote with great accuracy and discrimination. His language is not like that of Peter, picturesque but accurate and factual. He was not interested in presenting Jesus in relation to the past or the present, but rather to show his universality and inclusiveness. He described Jesus, not as Messiah or Lord, but as Saviour and Healer. Being a foreigner he was moved by the fact that Jesus had place in his kingdom for those not of his nationality or race. You find, therefore, in Luke the three parables of the lost sheep, the lost coin, and the lost son. Being a physician he was moved by the tenderness and the compassion of Jesus' dealing with women and children and aged folk. He pointed to the humanity of Jesus and his concern for man's physical well-being. You have, therefore, in his Gospel an emphasis upon Jesus healing the halt and the sick, the maimed and the blind.

John stresses light, life, love

The Gospel of John has a different approach. It was, perhaps, among the last books of the New Testament to be written, and it records the spiritual accents of Jesus' ministry. It was not written for a group or a class, but for all believers. No book ever written by man has been so critically studied, analyzed, or examined as the Gospel of John. The reason is simple: it makes such gigantic claims for Jesus. If the book can be discredited, these claims fall.

The Gospel of John places emphasis on eternal life. It bears witness to Jesus in three great words: light, life, and love. Jesus stands revealed in this Gospel, not as Messiah or King or Saviour, but as the incarnate Word of God which had become flesh. It relates Jesus to eternity and beyond time, and portrays our mystical oneness with Christ our Lord. It is a book for Christians. It concludes with, "These are written, that ye might believe that Jesus is the Christ, the Son of God; and that believing ye might have life through his name."

In going over the sermons which I have preached in the years of my ministry I discovered that I have preached more from the Gospel of John than from any other Gospel or book in the New Testament. That is perhaps as it should be.

Jesus is unique in history

Such, then, is the Jesus of history as we see him portrayed in the pages of the Gospels. What a romance that life holds! He was born in a borrowed cradle; he rode to triumph on a borrowed beast; he was buried in a borrowed grave. He was reared in poverty. He never traveled more than a hundred miles from home. He invented nothing; he discovered nothing; he constructed nothing; he destroyed nothing. The world at his death was the same as it had been externally at his birth. He made no important contacts. He never had a home of his own; he had no influential friends to plead his cause; he had no political leaders to intercede for him; he had no army to fight for him.

The friends of Jesus were among the humblest of earth —six of them came from a little fishing village of which his own countrymen knew but little. His father was a carpenter who died early; his mother was a humble peasant woman of Galilee. He had several brothers and some unnamed sisters. He spent the first thirty years of his life working at the bench of a village carpenter. For three years he went up and down the highways and byways of Palestine, healing, helping, teaching, and preaching. Of all men who ever trod this earth, "he saw life steadily and saw it whole."

Perhaps the most memorable quality which the disciples carried into their later lives about Jesus was his approach-ableness. He seemed to belong to them and become part of their day-by-day lives. He identified himself with his generation. He did not show the world a clenched fist after the manner of modern papier-mâché messiahs, but an outstretched arm. He did not build walls, but windows; not barricades, but bridges. He dragged the heartache and the tragedy of his generation across his soul. He identified himself with the paralytic whose body writhed in anguish, with the leper who had just enough feeling to know pain, with the blind who stumbled through the streets of eternal darkness, with the prodigal who stepped across the threshold of indiscretion. He was the most compassionate person who has ever lived.

There never lived a man who made such gigantic claims. He guaranteed to rewrite the history of the world. He determined to build an order without pain, without panic, without disease, and without sin. He said he would make men rethink life in terms of God. At a moment when the world was falling apart and nations were crumbling, he said, "And I, if I be lifted up from the earth, will draw all men unto me." He risked his reputation in order to

56

associate with outcasts and publicans. He staked the propagation of his gospel upon a handful of men whom Tacitus called illiterate and ignorant. There never lived a world figure who made such gigantic claims and proposed such dramatic changes.

Before he was thirty-three years of age, he had pitted against him the prejudices of organized religion. He died a disgraceful death, and when the Roman soldiers according to the custom of the times began to throw dice upon a flat stone before his cross to gamble for his possessions, he left them only a little cloak which his mother had woven for him in the uplands of Galilee. When he died, deserted by his disciples, it seemed as if his very name would disappear from history for all time. The Cross seemed an irretrievable disaster. To the disciples it marked the end of a dream.

Jesus is more than the Jesus of history

This is the picture of Jesus presented in the gospel narratives. But he is more than this. He is more than a figure in time; he is also a timeless figure. The Jesus of history is the Christ of experience. He lived, and he still lives. We do not worship a dead leader who lived in Palestine two thousand years ago. We worship a risen, living, exalted Lord. You can never explain Jesus in human terms. His life began and ended in a miracle. He is in time and yet beyond time. In him humanity and divinity meet. In him we see man at his best and God in his fullness. We see in him what man is capable of becoming. Calvary is the picture of man's wounded God.

It is true that some people stop with the humanity of Jesus. But the New Testament does not stop here. However difficult it may be, Jesus cannot be explained or understood in human terms. He is both Son of man and Son of God, perfect man and perfect God. In him God and man meet. In him the highest aspiration of man and the holiest revelation of God are joined together. He was divine-human in a unique sense. He was in the world but not of the world; he was in time and beyond time. Because he came from God and went to God, he had at his command forces and powers we cannot understand. He could do what no one else has ever done or ever will be able to do. Because I believe that, I have never found it difficult to accept the miracles of Jesus.

He still lives

Once upon a time he lived, but what is important for us is that he still lives. He is in the world today making, transforming, changing people in all races, languages, and lands. These constitute the fellowship of the twice-born, the redeemed by his grace. The story of that company began with the Acts of the Apostles, which is the record of the early Church with all its hopes and discouragements. If Christ had not risen from the grave, we would never have known him. The very birth of the Church came from the fact that Christ is still in the world today. He never took time into consideration. With him a thousand years were as a day. He never took geography into consideration. What he said, he meant for all lands and all languages. He is, therefore, not only the Jesus of history but the Christ of experience. He is at home in every century and country. He is part of the ongoing life of every generation and is eternally relevant.

> But warm, sweet, tender, even yet
>   A present help is he;
> And faith has still its Olivet,
>   And love its Galilee.

In John Masefield's play the wife of Pontius Pilate asks of a Roman soldier who took part in the crucifixion, "Do you think He is dead?"

The soldier replied, "No, lady, I don't."

"Then where is He?"

To this the soldier answered again, "Let loose in the world, lady, where neither Roman nor Jew can stop His truth."

His words ring out o'er land and sea

Today like bells of hope—resonant, harmonious, clear —the words of the soul's Saviour ring over land and sea. Sixty generations ago he walked this very earth, slept under stars that shine upon us, wondered at the glory of daybreak before which we, too, stand reverently. You may as well try to untwist moonbeams that fall with a mellow glow upon fields and forests as to suppose you can untwist the name and the memory of the Son of God from the heart of the ages. After twenty centuries that simple, artless story of his birth, life, and resurrection is read by more people than any other story of any other leader. It has been translated in over eleven hundred languages and dialects.

No argument against the sun can blot it from the sky, and no mole-eyed skepticism can wash from the memory of man the beauty of his glorious life. Tissot paints Jesus with the face of an Arab, Titian gives him the outline of an Italian, Murillo portrays him as a son of Spain, while Rubens gives him the features of a Flanders peasant. And yet we recognize him in all these settings. In Athens and in Antioch, in Rome and in Moscow, in Constantinople and in Washington, he is the same. And as the rising and waning moon draws to its heaving breast the tides of the sea in ebb and flow, so around the name of Jesus of Nazareth innumerable multitudes bow to confess him their

Lord and Master. Browning spoke the truth when he said, "That one Face, far from vanish, rather grows." The voice of humanity speaks in the simple lines:

> From the best bliss that earth imparts,
> We turn unfilled to thee again.

Jesus is the only character in history who holds his footing in innocence. He is the only figure in time whom you cannot place. He is the only religious leader whom the ages cannot dim. He is the only founder of a faith who satisfies the hope of the ages.

He is the solvent of every problem, every heartache, and every pain. He stands, the strong among the weak, the erect among the fallen, the pure among the unclean, the confident among the confused. The world is not done with him, but the world is done without him!

The Jesus of history and the Christ of experience will one day become the Christ triumphant. One day the kingdoms of this world will become the kingdom of our Lord and of his Christ. In that outburst of certain triumph the New Testament closes with the glorious lines which have fired the souls of men through the tumbling of the centuries, as John records them in Rev. 19:6. "Alleluia: for the Lord God omnipotent reigneth."

CHAPTER EIGHT

IN TIME AND BEYOND TIME

PEOPLE OFTEN ASK, "WHAT IS THE PRACTICAL VALUE of the Bible?" Here is a book written untold generations ago. What possible bearing can it have upon life in a world of which it never dreamed and never knew would exist? We are face to face with so many dilemmas and misgivings which were never faced by people who walk through the pages of the Book. We regard it with reverence and accept its authenticity, but is it relevant for our time?

The answer should not be too difficult to find. The Bible is the revealed Word of God and is, therefore, never outmoded or out of date. It has a meaning for the ongoing life of every generation. It comes to focus in every period of time. In it you will find an answer for every dilemma, every peril, every heartache, every pain—socially, politically, economically, and personally. Let us look at some of these dilemmas which disturb so many people today and which the Bible resolves.

The Book clears up our sense of futility

We belong to a generation which is overwhelmed by the sense of futility. To ever so many people the universe is a vast riddle, ending with a question mark and an exclamation point blistered over with tears. History seems to have no meaning. The universe has become a dead-end street. There is seemingly a lack of purpose in life. So much of this world does not make sense until one is tempted to repeat the lines in Faust, "The end of everything is nothing." Life is like a squirrel cage, going round and round but getting nowhere fast. We have motion but not direction. We are on the way, but we do not know where we are going. We are asked to play the game without knowing where the goal posts are. You do not have to live long to come upon these dilemmas and tensions. Does the Bible have an answer to this riddle of the universe, and can it resolve this sense of futility?

The Bible does not leave you in the dark very long on that issue. It fairly shouts the answer, Yes, from beginning to end. In the very opening of the Book you come upon, "And the evening and the morning were the first day." Many people today would not have written it in this fashion—they would have written it, "And the morning and the evening." But there it stands, and it is repeated five times. What does that mean? It makes the supreme affirmation that God's day does not end in night. God's day always ends in dawn. Darkness never speaks the last word. The universe has meaning, and history is coming out somewhere.

You come upon a similar assurance in the very center of the Bible when the prophet proclaims, "At evening time it shall be light." It closes with the assurance, "And there shall be no night there." The Bible does have the answer for those who have lost their footing. Issues in which God has a stake can never be permanently thwarted; they may be postponed, but they cannot be defeated. We live in a moral universe—what we sow we reap. This is not the kind of world in which it is one thing one day and something else another day. Pontius Pilate never speaks the last word. We hear our Lord say, "When ye shall hear of wars and commotions, be not terrified: . . .

for your redemption draweth nigh." There is a word in the New Testament which burns like a flame and shines like a star. It is the word "Maranatha"—"Jesus cometh." One day all things will be brought under his control, and the kingdoms of the world shall become the kingdom of our God and of his Christ. How relevant the message of the Bible is to this confused and bewildered age!

The Bible proves our lives mean something

There is another dilemma which confronts many people today. It is the lost sense of significance. They have made themselves believe that they do not count; there is no place of importance for them. Great movements are surging through the world, but they will never have part in them. New hopes are coming to mankind, but they are being bypassed. They imagine that they have nothing to contribute and seem mere victims of chance. What has the Bible to say about that?

The Word of God makes clear beyond the slightest shadow of doubt that the greatest accomplishments of history have come to pass by giving ordinary people extraordinary responsibilities. We are not victims of chance but children of God. Man is made in his image and fashioned after his likeness. Nobody can take that away from you. You may deface the image of God, but you can never efface it.

In a newspaper several years ago a cartoon appeared showing a soldier complete in full fighting equipment, his face obscured by the hideousness of a gas mask. Underneath were written these words, "So God created man in His own image." What a travesty this is upon the handiwork of God as revealed in the Bible!

The children of Israel in bondage in Egypt were mere slaves and scullions. All they could do was make brick without straw, yet God used these insignificant people to keep alive in the world a monotheistic faith, and they became one of the most significant people in history.

In the prophets, too, we see God speaking through human instruments chosen from varied walks of life. Most of them were humble men, but God filled them with his spirit and made use of them. Amos was a shepherd; Isaiah was a townsman in touch with the king's court and the wealthy noblemen of Jerusalem; Micah was a countryman whose love of his native land shines forth on every page of his book. Jeremiah came from a rustic background and influenced the whole history of Israel. Ezekiel was trained in the Temple at Jerusalem for the priesthood, but he was carried off to distant Babylon among his exiled countrymen. Across the flaming skies of Babylon he saw the awe-inspiring vision which made him a prophet of God. In the prophets you see what glory can come to humble people when they submit themselves to the will of God. They stood before kings and princes and were not afraid, even of death itself.

Look for a moment at the twelve disciples. What ordinary, commonplace men they were! For the most part they were ignorant and illiterate, without education and without influence. If they were living today, they would have a hard time breaking into respectable society. But when these simple people placed their lives at the disposal of God, they became founders of a new order. The little band has multiplied to one third of the population of the modern world. You hear Jesus give that assurance, "The very hairs of your head are all numbered." "If God so clothe the grass of the field, which to day is, and to morrow is cast into the oven, shall he not much more clothe you?" In no uncertain terms does the Bible answer this plaintive fear of life's insignificance.

The Book brings us peace of mind

Then, too, there is among people today a want of peace of mind. They seem frustrated and defeated. The sense of inadequacy makes them cynical and despairing. They have convinced themselves that hunger will always gnaw, disease will always ravage, and the four horsemen of the Apocalypse will always ride. They are sure that try though they may, everything will end in failure and despair.

Now carry that attitude which is so prevalent today to the open Book and you have the answer. Think of the Old Testament. Again and again God's promise to Abraham seemed incapable of being realized—that he would make of him a great nation. Abraham and Sarah were old, and they had no family. How could the promise be fulfilled? But the unexpected happened, and Isaac was born as the child of their old age. Jacob and his twelve sons left Canaan because of famine and went to sojourn in the land of Egypt, where their descendants became slaves and bondsmen. Was God's promise to be frustrated in this way? Then a leader arose in the person of Moses, who under the guidance of God led the children of Israel across the desert to the Promised Land. Surely now the promise was about to be fulfilled! But how could an untrained force of nomads stand against the military skill of the Canaanites? They were so near the goal and yet so far! But God was mindful of his people, and after a long and bitter struggle Israel conquered the land of Canaan.

Under David and Solomon, Israelite power attained its peak, but upon the death of Solomon came the breakup of the kingdom into north and south. Two hundred years later the northern kingdom fell to the Assyrians, and Israel went into exile, never to return. One hundred and fifty years later Judah succumbed to Babylonian power, and she, too, was forced into exile. God's plan seemed to have been completely thwarted. But no, a remnant returned. God was awake, keeping watch above his own. The plans of God march to their predestined end, "browbeat them though we may."

Jesus, too, was familiar with that experience. He went up and down healing the sick, giving sight to the blind, and making the lame to walk. He was always doing good, yet each effort was met with opposition and failure until at last he was sent to his cross. Golgotha scarred the souls of the disciples. It seemed the end of everything. But after three days he rose from the grave and lives forever. The New Testament gives the assurance that life may have a Calvary, but it will also have a resurrection.

The Book gives us security

There is another mood which prevails in the world today. It is the search for security. What most people want of life is to settle down in reasonable comfort, in a home, with work to do, with a reasonable income and a sense of permanence. Nations are struggling for this also. But what makes life secure? Upon what foundations does it rest?

There have been and there are false messiahs who offer mankind security. Yesterday the voice said, "Become a Nazi, and you will be secure and happy. Yield to my way, and you have nothing to fear of the world." But that hope has long ago been blasted. Nazism did not make good its claim; indeed, it brought an increasing sense of insecurity. Today another voice calls out, "Become a Communist, and all your problems will be solved. You will have money enough and food enough and clothing enough for all your wants." It proposes to build a new order upon economic determinism: security rests upon material things. Many people believe it. But behind the iron curtain there come signs of dismay; a growing number are fearful Communism cannot make good its claim. There is a third voice often heard today. It would have us believe that security of individuals and of nations rests upon political alliances, economic agreements, and military might. All this is wishful thinking. To heed that voice only leads to disillusionment.

Now carry this search for security to the Bible and see how it helps us in this quest. You soon discover the answer. The Bible establishes life upon the foundation of righteousness. Nations find safety not in economic determinism but in spiritual awareness. Security rests on moral values. When the finite is surrounded by the infinite and when the things of time are held in the embrace of a timelessness, then a sense of security comes to people. It is still true, "That nation alone is great whose God is the Lord." We are in the keeping of a God who holds us with a love that will not let us go. Mankind finds security in the assurance, "The foundation of God standeth sure, having this seal, The Lord knoweth them that are his." It was this conviction which Jesus made clear in his own life, "He that sent me is with me: the Father hath not left me alone."

The Book saves us from a sense of guilt

Then, too, our world is also desperately disturbed by the sense of guilt. The one question which people are asking today is, How can we get rid of sin? In the language of the Bible we ask, "What must I do to be saved?" In every life there is a sense of having missed the mark. We all fall short of some stature which we might have reached. The angels of our better selves are often smothered. Conscience makes us aware of the fact that we are not what we ought to be. Standing before the mirror, we look at life with a sense of shame and regret. Something seems to take possession of us, using our names, wearing our clothes, and driving us where we do not want to go. We may hide it from others, but we cannot hide it from ourselves. Life is burdened with a sense of guilt. We may rationalize it or analyze it or explain it, but we cannot explain it away. How can we get rid of sin?

The Bible has the final and sure answer, for it is the most realistic Book in all the world. It does not deny the fact. It does not look the other way. It does not gloss over our transgressions, nor does it sprinkle rose water over life's flaws. All sin is in reality a sin against God, "Against thee, thee only, have I sinned." Nowhere in the literature of the world will you find a more grim portrayal of sin in all its consequences.

But the Bible does something more than scold. Every page makes clear that when penitently and humbly we seek his forgiveness, he will grant it. "As far as the east is from the west, so far hath he removed our transgressions from us."

Whatever the Bible may or may not make clear, it always holds the incontestable assurance that God was in Christ reconciling the world unto himself. The central message of the Book is that deliverance from sin has been made possible and available. God in his infinite goodness has opened to us a door of escape from sin and fear and frustration. The Bible comes to focus in, "God so loved the world, that he gave his only begotten Son." The very heart of the Book is the offer of redemption.

The Book assures us of life after death

One finds also in our world the wistful search for some assurance of immortality. The old question is still asked today, "If a man die, shall he live again?" John Burroughs has spoken for so many, "I wish someone would light up the way for me." What has the Bible to say to that poignant question? The New Testament gives a clear and convincing answer. It lifts before the world the assurance that Jesus Christ rose from the grave. To the disciples Calvary seemed an irretrievable disaster. The last act of devotion on the part of his friends was to prepare his body for permanent interment. If they had believed he would rise again, they would have come to his grave with flowers and food. Then something happened.

Out of the gloom of the sepulcher in the garden of Joseph of Arimathea came the announcement that he had risen. And what is more, death had not changed him. He was familiar with their names and their problems. He was not a memory but an eternal presence, not a historical figure but an experience, not a figure in time but a timeless figure. And because he lives, so all who sleep in him shall be made alive. "As in Adam all die, even so in Christ shall all be made alive." "He that believeth in me, though he were dead, yet shall he live: and whosoever liveth and believeth in me shall never die." Standing wistful on the rim of the universe, wondering what has come of them, the Bible gives the assurance that we are not alone; because he lives, we shall live also.

The glory of the Bible is its relevance. It is at home in every age and country. Written untold centuries ago it is eternally contemporary. That is the Book of which Lincoln well said, "Accept all you can by reason, and the rest by faith; and you will live and die a better man."

CHAPTER NINE

A FINAL ASSURANCE

WE ALL SEARCH FOR SUSTAINING FORCES. LIFE NEEDS THE steadying sense of deep convictions which no storm can beat down and no darkness can dim. The tragedy of today is that people have no lee shore to which they can go in storms. Just before World War II someone came to see me. His whole life had tumbled in. The war had come in Europe, and he had lost everything: his home, his business, and all his possessions. He had just been able to escape with what he could carry. Then with his family he had to begin life all over again. The one thing which he wanted most was a philosophy by which he could rebuild his shattered life and dreams. Wistfully he was searching for God without calling him by that name. That is true of people everywhere. It lies at the basis of contemporary wistfulness.

Friends sustain us when things go wrong

Now there are many sustaining forces in life. You do not have to live long or travel far to know that many times we are sustained by friendship. More than one has lived bravely and uncomplainingly because he wanted to remain true to the end to some friend who believed in him and trusted him. When Elizabeth Barrett Browning was asked what was the secret of her life, she simply replied, "I had a friend." When things get out of hand and life tumbles in, when hope no longer sees a star, when the lights go out and the lamps of reason flicker, when it is touch and go, then to have near you someone who clasps your hand, saying, "I still believe in you; I still trust you," is to know one of the finest experiences this side the gates of paradise. What a benediction friendships are! I have had my share of them, and I will never cease to be grateful for them.

Health sustains us

We are often sustained by health. There are fortunate people who never know what it is to be weary. They never suffer from fatigue. There are inexhaustible resources of physical energy and reserves of well-being which seem never to run out. They have the physical strength to meet any experience and to endure any difficulty. That, too, is a precious gift of God which oftentimes we do not appreciate until we lose it for a while.

Material security sustains us

There are those who are sustained by material security. They never know the anxiety of, "What shall we eat?" or "What shall we drink?" or "Where withal shall we be clothed?" It is a simple fact that nine tenths of the lives of nine tenths of the people in the world turn on making a living. It is a grim business just to eke out an existence. There are fortunate people for whom that problem has been solved; they are independent and secure. This very security releases them from many anxieties and cares. It gives them peace and serenity.

A sense of belonging to a group sustains us

Sometimes we are sustained by the community. We feel ourselves part of a group or a company who travel the same road, who have the same interest, and who live by the same pattern. We have a sense of belonging; we are part of a movement or community. That, too, is a sustaining power. One day I talked to a soldier who had endured the agonizing experience of standing in a foxhole on Guadalcanal three days and three nights exposed to enemy fire, always cut off from his own troops and with his own rations exhausted. I asked him what it was that kept him going. He told me he kept thinking of those back home in the States who wanted to be free. He knew they were pulling for him and wanted him to stand brave and strong. It was a source of inestimable strength to him to be a part of the aspirations and hopes of a great nation. He was determined he would not let them down. So all of us, in one way or another, at one time or another, are sustained by the sense of belonging to a community.

But these are not enough

But these sustaining forces are never enough. There are times when friends fail, when health slips through our fingers, when our securities turn to ashes, and when the community seems to walk out on us. The person who is sustained only by these forces will find that life bowls him over at times. All these have their place, but they are not sufficient. A person may lack health, have no close friendships, know nothing of material security, walk alone, and still meet life bravely and buoyantly. The sustaining forces which are on the surface are never enough.

The Book gives us a sense of divine mission

I want to bear witness to those inner resources which never fail and by which one can meet the world unafraid. It is the golden text of my life. Years ago in a day of uncertainty and disillusionment, when my whole life seemed to be overwhelmed by forces beyond my control, one morning quite casually I opened my New Testament and my eyes fell upon this sentence, "He that sent me is with me—the Father hath not left me alone."

My life has never been the same since that hour. Everything for me has been forever different after that. I suppose that not a day has passed that I have not repeated it to myself. Many have come to me for counseling during these years, and I have always sent them away with this sustaining sentence. I have lived by this sentence, I have walked with it, and I have found in it my peace and strength. To me it is the very essence of religion. It lies at the rock bottom of everything that makes life worth living. Why is that? you ask.

1. Because I became convinced that there rests upon life a sense of divine mission. Through every episode and incident there runs some divine and eternal purpose. We are sent into this world. When Napoleon placed on the finger of Empress Josephine the wedding ring, he had engraved in it just two simple words: "To destiny." Well, around every life there runs this band of mission. We may meet each morning and each new experience with the conviction, "He sent me."

The first lesson of life is to find what that mission is. We have a strange way of rushing into life without asking first what place we are meant to fill. It is so easy to tumble headlong into something that is near at hand, but for which we may not be fitted. One of the perils of today is that we never take time to find out what we are fitted for. There are so many half failures and so many frustrations because people have not taken the time to inquire what God's purpose for them is. But whatever may be the purpose, it is well to know that life has a mission. We are here to play some role and to fulfill some specific task. We are not bits of flotsam or jetsam, carried by the tides upon the shores of a relentless fate. The very fact that we live implies we have a mission. Humanity is as a diamond; the individual is a facet on the diamond. It is our business to reflect something of the light and add glory to the whole.

The mission on which we are sent may not always be pleasant. It is quite possible to imagine ourselves at times in much more agreeable settings. It is not easy to fulfill one's mission. At times one is compelled to cry out in rebellion against some duty. Even Jesus shrank from his difficult mission when he cried in the garden, "Let this cup pass from me." It is not always an easy mission upon which life is sent. But we cannot walk out on life simply because it is difficult. God did not send us into this world to debate our mission but to fulfill it. "No man, having put his hand to the plow, and looking back, is fit for the kingdom of God."

You recall that day when Jesus told Peter what would be his mission. It happened on the dawn of that day on the shores of Galilee. This is what Jesus said: "When thou wast young, thou girdedst thyself, and walkedst whither thou wouldest: but when thou shalt be old, thou shalt stretch forth thy hands, and another shall gird thee, and carry thee whither thou wouldest not." That statement stunned Peter. He had not counted upon it. He did not want to say No, but neither was he prepared to say Yes. So he tried to evade the issue by saying, "Lord, and what shall this man do?" As if to say, "If this is to be my lot, what shall be the lot of this other disciple?" It is always so much easier to debate another's agreeable mission than to carry one's own cross. And yet you will never know joy or peace or strength until you live with that sense of mission, wherever it may lead, whatever it may require.

I have learned long since that to be true to one's duty

as God gives one light to see it brings one, in spite of everything, strange peace. It emancipates one from fear and from frustration. The person who lives with an inner sense of mission is never impatient, never petulant, never embittered. There is no such thing as defeat or failure possible on that basis. The assurance that God has sent you will put iron in your blood and fire the flames of faith. It is so that I have regarded my ministry.

It is a great thing so to live that every morning you may go out into the world with the conviction that you have been sent on some divine errand. You are not held responsible for the conclusions of that mission, but you are held responsible for facing it.

The Book gives us a sense of divine presence

2. It taught me that life is sustained also by a sense of divine presence. *"The Father hath not left me alone."* When we put our feet upon the road, we do not go it alone; he travels with us. When life begins its long pilgrimage through the earth, God does not bow himself out of it. On the shores of every lake and sea there are boats and scows which have been abandoned and left like gaunt skeletons buried in the sand. But on the shores of eternity there are no abandoned lives. The Almighty does not launch our little boats and then set us adrift in a cruel sea. The unwearying Shepherd always goes before and leads his flock. There is no depth so deep, no height so inaccessible, and no distance so great that it escapes his notice. The psalmist was right, "If I make my bed in hell, behold, thou art there." When night closes in and the world tumbles apart, when things get out of hand, when all the lights fail and no friend is near, then there is a voice which sounds like the far-off waterfalls, saying, "Lo, I am with you alway."

We may put down as a profound assurance that nothing shall separate us from the love of God that is in Christ Jesus. He is able to keep that which we have committed unto him against that day. There are relentless and cruel forces which play upon our lives. Circumstances force themselves upon us for which we are not responsible and over which we have no control. Sooner or later experiences like that come to every human life. In an hour like that it is so easy to suppose that we are alone. The classic illustration of all that is Elijah sitting under a juniper tree lifting the bitter wail, "I, even I only, am left; and they seek my life, to take it away." There is a good deal of that in the world today. One often comes upon this horticultural lamentation, and it leads to such fear, disillusionment, and frustration. It embitters life and poisons the very roots of our being. Faith flickers like some smoking lamp. The universe becomes meaningless. There is no place for that philosophy in the Christian religion. Upon whatever errand we may be sent, we always have the unfailing presence of an unfaltering God.

How can you say you are alone when the centuries fight for you, when eternity is on your side, and when you are in the keeping of a God who holds you with a love that will not let you go? As surely as the spirit of God brooded over the troubled waters of creation until order came out of chaos, and as surely as Christ walked down the road of Emmaus with the bewildered pilgrims, so surely does his presence go with you. You worship a God who is too good to forget you and too great to let you drift. In every experience, however blistering, and in every hour, however dark, you may say, "I am not alone."

These two convictions did not originate with me. I did not think them up. These words were spoken by our Lord himself. Jesus gave them to the world and bore witness to them in his own life. Over the broken waves of the sea of life comes the golden glow: "Follow me. Lo, I am with you alway." He will not fail us if we do not fail him. The Bible has the answer.

NOTES

Page	Line	
38	2	I Sam. 3:10
38	7	I Sam. 3:9
38	15	Amos 7:15
40	1	John 1:14
40	4	Matt. 1:23
40	7	Heb. 1:1-2
40	15	John 20:31
45	12	Job 19:25
46	19	Amos 5:24
46	23	Isa. 6:3
47	29	Ps. 51:17
48	6	John 1:29
48	12	Eccl. 9:5
48	13	Eccl. 3:19
48	20	I Cor. 15:20, 22
49	4	Matt. 5:33-34
52	9	John 9:25
52	10	I John 1:1, 3
55	12	John 20:31
56	33	John 12:32
58	29	John Greenleaf Whittier
62	14	Gen. 1:5
62	24	Zech. 14:7
62	25	Rev. 22:5
62	33	Luke 21:9, 28
63	3	I Cor. 16:22
64	29	Luke 12:7
64	30	Matt. 6:30
67	17	II Tim. 2:19
67	20	John 8:29
68	10	Ps. 51:4
68	16	Ps. 103:12
68	25	John 3:16
69	16	I Cor. 15:22
69	17	John 11:25-26
73	3	John 8:29
74	11	Matt. 26:39
74	15	Luke 9:62
74	20	John 21:18
74	27	John 21:21
75	28	Ps. 139:8
75	32	Matt. 28:20
76	11	I Kings 19:10

DATE DUE

APR 1 5			
APR 1 '86			
DEC 19 1988			
GAYLORD			PRINTED IN U.S.A.